How to Take Notes

at Church

BY

RALPH SMITH

DEDICATION

This book is dedicated to a very special man of God. His name is Alfred D. Harvey Jr., and he is the pastor of one of the fastest growing churches in the Midwest. He has been a great example to me of a husband, Pastor, and a believer. One of the greatest traits I've learned from Pastor Harvey is his ability to be patient, while waiting on God (*which means continually serving*) when making a decision. **Thank you** for your boldness, dedication, and your commitment to excellence!

First and foremost I want to thank you for buying this book. **Thank you!** If this book came into your life by some other avenue like in the form of a (gift), my appreciation is still directed toward you, because by reading this book you have given me an opportunity to speak into your life. I am excited for you and for the person you will become as you benefit from this information. I truly believe that this information will add to your life in more ways than you can ever imagine. After reading this book, you will have some insight on a retrieval process for gathering information at church or for listening to the Word of God being taught on cassette tape, VHS, CD, or via the television while sitting at home.

May God bless you with understanding,

Ralph Smith

TABLE OF CONTENTS

THE PURPOSE BEHIND THE BOOK

For the sake of this discussion or study we will define "Church" as the place where the Body of Christ and those desiring to enter the Body of Christ go and hear the Word of God proclaimed. In **Matthew 4:4** Jesus said that, *"Man shall...live...by every word that proceedeth out of the mouth of God."* This is very interesting because God has brought us to a point in history, as never before, where a person can receive the Word of God from many different avenues. For example, in the last twenty-five years Christian conferences of all types have been on the rise. There are more ministries now using radio and television as an avenue than ever before, and in addition to this the local church where every citizen of the Kingdom of God should be an <u>active</u> participant is still training the people of God for effective leadership. Along with all these different ways to spread the Gospel, I must also add audiocassette, VHS, CD, and in some cases DVD. Now, if I have failed to mention other avenues, like the publishing of Christian material or the Internet, please forgive me. Nevertheless it only reaffirms that once everything that is said is done, you and I will be left with no excuse.

I must admit that the title, as well as the way the information in this book, will be presented, is directed toward the local church. But if you can understand the principles contained within this book, the information will help you wherever you have chosen to listen to the Word of God.

Romans 10:17 *So then faith cometh by hearing, and hearing by the Word of God.*

I believe that every local church should be a teaching ministry that is committed to equipping the saints, and anyone who walks through its doors, with successful living principles derived from the Word of God. It should always be their objective to share *TRUTH* that is applicable, institutional and understandable. To accomplish this task, it is quite evident that every church should strongly recommend the bringing of a Bible, notebook, pencil/pen, and a highlighter (*optional*) to every service. "Although I believe these tools are much needed for any student of the Word of God to be successful, I do not assume that they understand the way in which to use them." These were the words I quoted to the Youth Pastor of my church, where I was an active participant. The youth department (*teenagers particularly*) was one of the areas in which I voluntarily served. I and the other active participants who also served in the same auxiliary were meeting one Saturday with our Youth Pastor on ways we could effectively meet the spiritual needs of the teens. We wanted to make sure that we were doing everything possible to produce the greatest opportunity for them to understand the Word deposit they were receiving.

Our pastor had already established rules for us to make sure that every teen that comes through the doors of Teen Church have a Bible, notebook, pencil/pen, and a highlighter (*optional*). As we were going over these rules, the Holy Spirit spoke to my heart and said; "*Although these tools are needed, never assume they know how to use them.*" I recited those words back to the Youth Pastor that day and that was the beginning of thoughts concerning this project. Then after a series of events, I meditated more and more on those words spoken to me from the Holy Spirit and concluded that He was not only referring to the teens at my church, but the Body of Christ as a whole.

There are many people who walk through the doors of a church, and everyone's background is somewhat different. Because of this, I believe it is our duty to share with them some natural things which will aid them in gaining spiritual truths. This book is set up to meet one of those purposes. I truly believe that the following information will help you maximize your opportunity to fully understand the Word deposit that is being planted in your life, wherever you have chosen to hear the Word of God. As you well know, this book is entitled, *How to Take Notes at Church*, so let me say this before I continue. If you go to church on a regular basis (*and you should*) and you never have anything to note, then I would seriously reconsider that particular place of spiritual training and redevelopment you have chosen to attend!

I, ME, MINE

READ:
Philippians 2:1-11

Let nothing be done
through selfish
ambition or conceit.
—Philippians 2:3

THE BIBLE IN ONE YEAR:
■ 1 Chronicles 13–15
■ John 7:1-27

In 1970, the Beatles began work on a documentary intended to show how their music was made. But instead of revealing the process of musical creativity, the film pulled the curtain back on a display of self-interest and bickering. The band members were more concerned about their own songs than the advancement of the group. Shortly after the project was completed, the group dissolved in disharmony and broken friendships.

It's an age-old problem. In the first century AD, the apostle Paul feared that the believers in the church at Philippi would fall into the trap of selfishness. He knew that when the desire for personal advancement overrides concern for one another, attitudes quickly become disruptive and divisive.

To counteract this dangerous tendency, Paul wrote, "Let nothing be done through selfish ambition or conceit, but in lowliness of mind let each esteem others better than himself. Let each of you look out not only for his own interests, but also for the interests of others" (Phil. 2:3-4).

What would a documentary of your life reveal? Selfishness or selflessness? We must look out for one another, for selfless concern will prevent division and build unity in our church families. —Bill Crowder

Lord, let me live from day to day
In such a self-forgetful way
That even when I kneel to pray
My prayer will be for others. —Meigs

A heart that is focused on others
will not be consumed with self.

I SHALL NOT WANT

READ:
James 4:1-10

The world is Mine,
and all its fullness.
—Psalm 50:12

THE BIBLE IN ONE YEAR:
■ 1 Chronicles 16–18
■ John 7:28-53

Before they were a week old, the eaglets were fighting over food. Neither was strong enough to hold up his head for more than a few seconds, so the pair looked like fuzzballs with bobble-heads attached. But whenever the parents brought food to the nest, the bigger eaglet was quick to peck down his brother to keep him from getting a single bite. His aggression would have been understandable if food was scarce, or if the parents couldn't be trusted to supply what he needed. But nothing could be further from the truth. The eaglets were being fed fish many times their size; there was more than enough for both of them.

The greedy eaglet reminds me of our own foolishness when we try to get for ourselves something that belongs to someone else (James 4:1-5). Conflicts erupt because we want something that God has given to a friend, colleague, relative, or neighbor. Instead of asking God for what we need, we try to get what He's given to someone else (v.2). But God has something good for each of us. We don't need what belongs to anyone else. And we certainly never need to harm anyone to get what we need.

Our loving heavenly Father has more than enough for everyone. —Julie Ackerman Link

The secret of contentment is
To let the Lord supply;
Just do your part and put God first
And on His Word rely. —D. De Haan

Our needs will never exhaust God's supply.

TOXIC LOOK-ALIKES

READ:
Acts 8:9-23

Your heart is not right in the sight of God. Repent therefore of this your wickedness.
—Acts 8:21-22

THE BIBLE IN ONE YEAR:
- Jeremiah 6–8
- 1 Timothy 5

Our yard makes poison ivy happy. I learned this the hard way. Even though I was being careful, I came in contact with the plant and ended up with a nasty, itchy rash.

Poison ivy looks like many harmless plants, and it keeps company with some beautiful ones. One gardener couldn't figure out why she got poison ivy whenever she pruned her roses. She later discovered that a poison ivy vine was taking advantage of the tender loving care she gave to her rosebush.

Some people are like toxic plants. They look harmless, and they blend in with people who, like roses, are fragrant and beautiful.

Simon the sorcerer fit this description. He followed Philip and was baptized, but then he asked to buy the ability to lay hands on people so they could receive the Holy Spirit. Peter was appalled at his request and urged him to repent (Acts 8:22).

Sometimes people use the favorable environment of a healthy church as a network for selfish purposes. Like poison ivy among roses, they cause much misery. Like Simon, anyone who does this needs to repent, and everyone else needs to avoid contact with such a person. Spiritual look-alikes appear good but their "fruit" is toxic. —Julie Ackerman Link

A PRAYER:
Help me, Lord, to be discerning and not let others lead me astray with their falsehood. May the fruit of my life be an example of a follower of Christ. Amen.

A false life belies a true faith.

DECLARATION OF DEPENDENCE

READ:
John 15:1-8

Without Me you can do nothing. —John 15:5

THE BIBLE IN ONE YEAR:
- Jeremiah 9–11
- 1 Timothy 6

Adults celebrate when children learn to do something on their own: get dressed, brush their teeth, tie shoelaces, ride a bike, walk to school.

As adults, we like to pay our own way, live in our own houses, make our own decisions, rely on no outside help. Faced with an unexpected challenge, we seek out "self-help" books. All the while we are systematically sealing off the heart attitude most desirable to God and most descriptive of our true state in the universe. It's what Jesus told His disciples: "Without Me you can do nothing" (John 15:5).

The truth is that we live in a web of dependence, at the center of which is God, in whom all things hold together. Norwegian theologian Ole Hallesby settled on the single word *helplessness* as the best summary of the heart attitude that God accepts as prayer. He said, "Only he who is helpless can truly pray."

Most parents feel a pang when the child outgrows dependence, even while knowing the growth to be healthy and normal. With God, the rules change. We never outgrow dependence, and to the extent we think we do, we delude ourselves. Prayer is our declaration of dependence upon the Lord. —Philip Yancey

> *Give Him each perplexing problem,*
> *All your needs to Him make known;*
> *Bring to Him your daily burdens—*
> *Never carry them alone! —Adams*

Pray as if your life depended upon it. It does!

EMERGENCY KIT

READ:
Ephesians 6:10-18

Therefore take up the whole armor of God, that you may be able to withstand in the evil day, and having done all, to stand.
—Ephesians 6:13

THE BIBLE IN ONE YEAR:
■ Jeremiah 15–17
■ 2 Timothy 2

For a dozen years, I took an auto emergency kit on every long driving trip but never had to use it. It became such a familiar item that on the night we really needed it, I forgot it was there. But fortunately my wife remembered.

After hitting a deer on a dark rural highway, our van was completely disabled. While I fumbled with a small flashlight to assess the damage and call a tow truck, my wife opened the emergency kit, set out a reflective warning marker, then turned on the bright flashlight, much to my surprise. Later we talked about how a crisis can cause us to forget the resources we have, just when we need them most.

Paul urged the Ephesians to "put on the whole armor of God, that you may be able to stand against the wiles of the devil" (Eph. 6:11). This protective covering includes truth, righteousness, readiness, faith, salvation, and prayer (vv.14-18). Although these spiritual resources guard us each day, we need to remember them when disaster strikes and the enemy tries to undermine our confidence in God's love and care.

Use the kit. "Take up the whole armor of God, that you may be able to withstand in the evil day, and having done all, to stand" (v.13). —David McCasland

When Satan launches his attack,
We must take heart and pray;
If we submit ourselves to God,
He'll be our strength and stay. —Sper

God provides the armor, but we must put it on.

October 27
Wednesday

A LOCK OF HAIR

READ:
Judges 16:4-17

The LORD . . . [shows]
Himself strong on
behalf of those whose
heart is loyal to Him.
—2 Chronicles 16:9

THE BIBLE IN ONE YEAR:
■ Jeremiah 12–14
■ 2 Timothy 1

After his return from the moon, Neil Armstrong was often plagued by the media. Seeking greater privacy, he moved his family into a small town. But notoriety was a nuisance even there. Armstrong's barber found out that people would pay good money to get a lock of his hair. So after giving the space hero several haircuts, he sold the clippings to a buyer for $3,000! Armstrong was shocked at the barber's disloyalty.

The Scriptures tell of another story of disloyalty and a haircut. As a symbol of God's calling of Samson as a Nazirite, he was never to cut his hair (Judg. 13:5). When the Spirit of God came upon him, he was given superhuman strength over his enemies (15:14). Wanting to overpower him, the Philistines hired Delilah, a woman who had a relationship with him, to find out the secret of that strength. He foolishly told her that his power would be gone if his hair were cut. She lulled him to sleep and had him shorn (16:5,19).

Greed can drive us to be disloyal to others and to God, causing us to make sinful choices. Our desire should be to exhibit a heart that is fully committed to love the Lord and others. He shows "Himself strong on behalf of those whose heart is loyal to Him" (2 Chron. 16:9). —Dennis Fisher

O Lord, may my heart be loyal to You
In all that I say and all that I do;
When a trusted person is not a true friend,
I know that on You I can always depend. —Hess

Loyalty is the test of true love.

STOCKPILING OR STORING?

READ:
Ecclesiastes 5:8-17

_____

Just exactly as he came,
so shall he go.
—Ecclesiastes 5:16

THE BIBLE IN ONE YEAR:
■ Jeremiah 24–26
■ Titus 2

Rugs, lamps, a washer and dryer, even the food in the cupboards—everything was for sale! My husband and I stopped at an estate sale one day and wandered through the house, overwhelmed by the volume of belongings. Dish sets littered the dining room table. Christmas decorations filled the front hallway. Tools, toy cars, board games, and vintage dolls crowded the garage. When we left, I wondered if the homeowners were moving, if they desperately needed money, or if they had passed away.

This reminded me of these words from Ecclesiastes: "Just exactly as he came, so shall he go" (5:16). We're born empty-handed and we leave the world the same way. The stuff we buy, organize, and store is ours only for a while—and it's all in a state of decay. Moths munch through our clothes; even gold and silver may not hold their value (James 5:2-3). Sometimes "riches perish through misfortune" (Eccl. 5:14), and our kids don't get to enjoy our possessions after we're gone.

Stockpiling possessions in the here-and-now is foolish, because we can't take anything with us when we die. What's important is a proper attitude toward what we have and how we use what God has given. That way we'll be storing up our treasure where it belongs—in heaven. —Jennifer Benson Schuldt

> _Whatever we possess on earth_
> _We have to leave behind;_
> _But everything we give to God_
> _In heaven we will find._ —Sper

**Letting go of earthly possessions
enables us to take hold of heavenly treasure.**

COMPLETELY CLEAN

READ:
Hebrews 10:1-18

It is not possible that the blood of bulls and goats could take away sins. —Hebrews 10:4

THE BIBLE IN ONE YEAR:
■ Jeremiah 22–23
■ Titus 1

Happy birthday to me. Happy birthday to me. Happy birthday to me-ee. Happy birthday to me. . . . Happy bir . . .

After humming the "birthday song" a second time, I turned off the faucet's running water. It is said that singing the song through twice while washing your hands (about 20 seconds) is a good way to remove most bacteria. But it doesn't last. I need to repeat this process each time they are contaminated.

In the Old Testament, the people of God offered sacrifices over and over to cover their sins. But the blood of the animals didn't actually "take away sins" (Heb. 10:11). Only the precious sacrifice of Jesus could do that!

Animal sacrifices are no longer needed because Christ's sacrifice . . .

• *was once for all*—unlike animal sacrifices, which had to be offered "continually year by year" (vv.1-3,10).

• *cleanses us completely from all guilt and sin*—unlike the blood of animals that was a reminder of sin's penalty and could never take away our sins (vv.3-6,11).

"By one offering [Christ] has perfected forever those who are being sanctified" (v.14). Only through Jesus can we be declared completely clean. —Cindy Hess Kasper

Once for all, O sinner, receive it;
Once for all, O brother, believe it;
Cling to the cross, the burden will fall,
Christ hath redeemed us once for all. —Bliss

Christ's cleansing power
can remove the most stubborn stain of sin.

NEIGHBORLY KINDNESS

READ:
Luke 10:25-37

A certain Samaritan, as he journeyed, came where he was. And when he saw him, he had compassion.
—Luke 10:33

THE BIBLE IN ONE YEAR:
■ Jeremiah 27–29
■ Titus 3

One of the major obstacles to showing compassion is making prejudgments about who we think is worthy of our compassion. Jesus told a parable to answer the question: "Who is my neighbor?" (Luke 10:29). Or, who qualifies as worthy of our neighborly acts?

Jesus told of a man who traveled on the notoriously dangerous road from Jerusalem to Jericho. As he traveled, he fell among thieves and was robbed, beaten, and left for dead. Religious Jews (a priest and a Levite) passed him, but they walked by on the other side, probably for fear of being religiously defiled. But a Samaritan came along and had unconditional compassion on the wounded stranger.

Jesus' audience would have gasped at this because Jews despised Samaritans. The Samaritan could have limited or qualified his compassion because the man was a Jew. But he did not limit his neighborly kindness to those he thought were worthy. Instead, he saw a human being in need and resolved to help him.

Are you limiting your kindness to the ones you deem worthy? As followers of Jesus, let us find ways to show neighborly kindness to all people, especially to those we have judged as unworthy. —Marvin Williams

How many lives shall I touch today?
How many neighbors will pass my way?
I can bless so many and help so much,
If I meet each one with a Christlike touch. —Jones

Our love for Christ is only as real
as our love for our neighbor.

It Can Never Happen To Me

READ:
Psalm 30:6-12

Now in my prosperity I said, "I shall never be moved." —Psalm 30:6

THE BIBLE IN ONE YEAR:
■ Jeremiah 30–31
■ Philemon

Actor Christopher Reeve was paralyzed in a horseback riding accident in 1995. Prior to this tragedy, he had played the part of a paraplegic in a movie. In preparation, Reeve visited a rehabilitation facility. He recalled: "Every time I left that rehab center, I said, 'Thank God that's not me.'" After his accident, Reeve regretted that statement: "I was so setting myself apart from those people who were suffering without realizing that in a second that could be me." And sadly, for him, it was.

We too may look at the troubles of others and think that it could never happen to us. Especially if our life journey has led to a measure of success, financial security, and family harmony. In a moment of vanity and self-sufficiency, King David admitted to falling into the trap of feeling invulnerable: "Now in my prosperity I said, 'I shall never be moved'" (Ps. 30:6). But David quickly caught himself and redirected his heart away from self-sufficiency. He remembered that he had known adversity in the past and God had delivered him: "You have turned for me my mourning into dancing" (v.11).

Whether He has brought us blessing or trial, God still deserves our gratitude and trust. —Dennis Fisher

I can always count on God, my heavenly Father,
For He changes not; He always is the same;
Yesterday, today, forever, He is faithful,
And I know He loves me, praise His holy name. —Felten

In good times and bad, our greatest need is God.

May 20
Thursday

A WORTHY OFFERING

READ:
Genesis 4:1-7

If you do well, will you not be accepted? And if you do not do well, sin lies at the door.
—Genesis 4:7

THE BIBLE IN ONE YEAR:
■ 1 Chronicles 10–12
■ John 6:45-71

I was delighted when a mutual friend gave my neighbor a Bible. But my neighbor told me she stopped reading it because she couldn't understand why God would be so unfair as to reject Cain's offering. "After all," she said, "as a farmer, he simply brought to God what he had. Did God expect him to buy a different kind of sacrifice?" Sadly, she had missed the point.

It wasn't that God didn't like vegetables. Rather, He knew that Cain's offering was masking an unrighteous attitude. Cain wasn't fully committed to God, as expressed by the fact that he wasn't living according to His ways.

It's easy to worship God on the outside while stubbornly keeping territory from Him on the inside. Jude writes about outwardly religious people who use religious activities to cover the reality of their sinful lives: "Woe to them! For they have gone the way of Cain" (Jude 11). We can faithfully serve God, sing His praises, and give sacrificially to His work. But God doesn't want any of that without our hearts.

Does the Lord take priority over our plans and dreams? Is He worth more than the sin that tempts us? When we express to Him that He is more worthy than anything or anyone else in our lives, it's an offering He won't refuse. —Joe Stowell

Lord, may our worship and our praise,
From hearts surrendered to Your ways,
Be worthy offerings of love
For all Your blessings from above. —Sper

God won't refuse a heart that is surrendered to Him.

SECONDHAND FAITH

READ:
Judges 2:6-12

Another generation arose after them who did not know the LORD nor the work which He had done for Israel.
—Judges 2:10

THE BIBLE IN ONE YEAR:
■ 1 Chronicles 7–9
■ John 6:22-44

When I was growing up in Singapore, I remember that some of my school friends were kicked out of their homes by their non-Christian parents for daring to believe in Jesus Christ. They suffered for their beliefs and emerged with stronger convictions. By contrast, I was born and raised in a Christian family. Though I didn't suffer persecution, I too had to make my convictions my own.

The Israelites who first entered the Promised Land with Joshua saw the mighty acts of God and believed (Judg. 2:7). But sadly, the very next generation "did not know the LORD nor the work which He had done for Israel" (v.10). So it was not long before they turned aside to worship other gods (v.12). They didn't make their parents' faith their own.

No generation can live off the faith of the previous generation. Every generation needs a firsthand faith. When faced with trouble of any kind, the faith that is not personalized is likely to drift and falter.

Those who are second, third, or even fourth generation Christians have a wonderful legacy, to be sure. However, there's no secondhand faith! Find out what God says in His Word and personalize it so that yours is a fresh, firsthand faith (Josh. 1:8). —C. P. Hia

> *O for a faith that will not shrink*
> *Though pressed by many a foe,*
> *That will not tremble on the brink*
> *Of any earthly woe!* —Bathurst

If your faith is not personalized, it's not faith.

A Parable Of Forgiveness

A beautiful perspective on forgiveness is given to us in Jesus' well-known story of the prodigal son in Luke 15:11-31. Here we see evidence of:

A Repentant Heart. The prodigal son demonstrated a repentant heart that was broken when he came to his senses and decided to return home to his father. Repentance is a brokenness and change of life-direction marked by:

• *Hunger for restoration*. He longed for something more than what he had available to him in his sin. He longed to go home (v.16).

• *Humble confession*. He willingly acknowledged his selfish violation of love, first toward God and then toward others (vv.18-19).

• *Plea for mercy*. He recognized that he deserved nothing and pleaded for mercy, to serve as a slave, without a demand for restoration to his previous position in the family (v.21).

A Forgiving Heart. It is the father in the story who represents the unexpected forgiving heart of God in response to genuine repentance that is marked by:

• *Hopeful anticipation*. The father never gave up hoping for his son's repentance and return home to be restored to him again. He was persevering in prayer and intently looking for the day he saw the familiar form of his son on the horizon (v.20). The hopeful yearning for restoration was never quenched in the heart of the father.

• *Courageous love*. The father was willing to humble himself and not conform to the cultural mandate of his day to make his son grovel in the dirt. Instead, in a spontaneous, jubilant act of love, he ran to embrace his son (v.20).

- *Gracious mercy.* Forgiveness was joyfully granted because he sensed the repentance in the heart of his son, and he restored him to a position of sonship that was unheard of (v.22).

- *Celebration of repentance.* The father planned a party to celebrate the return of his son. His son was heading in a direction that brought separation and death to their relationship, but now he was alive and reconciled to his father (vv.23-24).

An Unforgiving Heart. The older son (representative of the Pharisees who were listening to the parable) is a study in the stubborn refusal to forgive that is characterized by:

- *Hardness.* There was an unwillingness on his part to consider restoration of his younger foolish brother. He felt justifiably cold toward his brother. And he was outraged that his father would still want a relationship with a son who had so deeply offended him (v.28).

- *Demanding of revenge.* His focus was only on immediately punishing his brother for what he had done rather than focusing on what had changed in his heart. He wanted to make his brother pay for what he had done. He had no mercy and no desire for reconciliation (v.28).

- *Arrogant refusal to celebrate.* The older son withheld relationship from both his brother and his father (v.28). He missed an opportunity for joy and celebration because he was preoccupied with himself. He missed the loving heart of the father that longs for restoration. Instead, he angrily withdrew in self-justified indignation and smugness over being right, and he refused to recognize that what he was doing was causing just as much pain and separation between himself and his father as was caused by his younger brother.

The refusal to forgive indicates a rebellious, stubborn heart that has not drunk deeply of the water of grace and mercy at the well of God's forgiveness (Luke 7:47).

Our unwillingness to love those who have harmed us reflects our own failure to understand how much God has loved us. The apostle Peter reminded us of this in the first chapter of his second New Testament letter. After describing seven essential, progressive graces, which culminate in godliness, brotherly kindness, and love (2 Peter 1:5-7), he added, "For if these things are yours and abound, you will be neither barren nor unfruitful in the knowledge of our Lord Jesus Christ. For he who lacks these things is shortsighted, even to blindness, and has forgotten that he was cleansed from his old sins" (vv.8-9).

This ability to love and forgive can begin only when we have first been forgiven by God. Have you taken that first step?

Adapted from *When Forgiveness Seems Impossible,* © 2001. You may read the booklet on the Web at **www.discoveryseries.org/cb941**

TOPIC INDEX
December • January • February 2011–2012

WHY TAKE NOTES?

As I stated earlier, the bringing of a Bible, notebook, pencil/pen, and highlighter (*optional*) to every service you attend should be as automatic as you bringing your tithes and offerings to church. Never ever come to church empty-handed! Your participation in the service is just as important to your potential in receiving the information as it is to the sower (*minister*) who was sent to give you that information. In Ephesians 4:11, there is a list of offices that have been termed by biblical Scholars as the Five-fold Ministry (Apostles, Prophets, Evangelists, Pastors, and Teachers), but the purposes for these offices are listed in the verses that follow:

Ephesians 4:12-14, *For the perfecting of the saints, for the work of the ministry, for the edifying of the body of Christ: (13) Till we all come in the unity of the faith, and of the knowledge of the Son of God, unto a perfect man, unto the measure of the stature of the fullness of Christ: (14) That we henceforth be no more children, tossed to and fro, and carried about with every wind of doctrine, by the sleight of men, and cunning craftiness, whereby they lie in wait to deceive;*

God has set up a system that operates through the Lord Jesus Christ that is intended to build you up into spiritual maturity. This is what Paul was referring to in verse 13 above when he said, "*Unto a perfect man.*" The best and safest way to get to know God is to learn about Him through His Word. **2 Timothy 3:16 and 17** declare that:

ALL scripture is given by inspiration of God, and is profitable for doctrine, for reproof, for correction, for instruction in righteousness: That the man of God may be perfect (**spiritually mature**) *thoroughly furnished unto all good works.*

So, as you can see, hearing the Word of God is extremely vital and essential to your spiritual growth. Let me say it this way: it is impossible, I repeat <u>impossible</u> for you to grow in the things of God without the Word of God. Whenever a minister of the Gospel teaches the Word of God, he is literally presenting God to you and not just the Word of God to you!

John 1:1, *In the beginning was the Word, and the Word was with God, and the Word was God.*

Before I share with you some reasons why you should take notes, let me give you a few more scriptures to meditate on that reveal just how important the Word of God should be to you:

Numbers 23:19, *God is not a man, that he should lie; neither the son of man, that he should repent: hath he said, and shall he not do it? or hath he spoken, and shall he not make it good?*

Joshua 23:14, *And, behold, this day I am going the way of all the earth: and ye know in all your hearts and in all your souls, that not one thing* *hath failed of all the good things which the Lord your God spake concerning you; all are come to pass unto you, and not one thing hath failed thereof.*

Psalm 33:9, *For he spake, and it was done; he commanded, and it stood fast.*

Isaiah 55:8-11, *For my thoughts are not your thoughts, neither are your ways my ways, saith the Lord. For as the heavens are higher than the earth, so are my ways higher than your ways, and my thoughts than your thoughts. For as the rain cometh down, and the snow from heaven, and returneth not thither, but watereth the earth, and maketh it bring forth and bud, that it may give seed to the sower, and bread to the eater: So shall my word be that goeth forth out of my mouth: it shall not return unto me void, but it shall accomplish that which I please, and it shall prosper in the thing whereto I sent it.*

Mark 13:31, *Heaven and earth shall pass away: but my words shall not pass away.*

John 17:17, *Sanctify them through thy truth: thy word is truth.*

2 Corinthians 1:20, *For all the promises of God in him are yea, and in him Amen, unto the glory of God by us.*

Hebrews 11:3, *Through faith we understand that the worlds were framed by the word of God, so that things which are seen were not made of things which do appear.*

I could go on, but I think that is enough to give you a starting point on your journey to discovering just how important the Word of God is to you. This is why I believe that attending church on a regular basis is a trademark for successful Christians. If you want to take it a step further and be really used by God, try listening to the Word of God every day, then you will not only be a Christian, but an uncommon Christian! From this point on I'm going to assume that you desire to be an uncommon Christian, and give you some reasons why you should take notes when listening to the Word of God.

1) **Taking notes will help you remember what is being taught, so that your examination process will be effective.**

This is vital for a number of reasons, but let me share with you, which I believe is the most important. In **Ephesians 4:14** the Word of God tells us that God does not want us to be deceived (paraphrased). If you did not know, it is your responsibility to make sure that the information you are receiving is correct. I call it the examination process. You are the first gatekeeper of your own heart. **Proverbs 4:23** says **Keep thy heart with all diligence; for out of it are the issues of life**. There are three gates to your heart:

1. Your eyes
2. Your ears
3. Your mouth

Because of this, (1) you must be careful what you see, (2) judge what you hear in light of the Scriptures, and (3) discern what you are ready and willing to repeat out of your mouth.

Remember, if it gets in your heart in abundance, it will eventually come out of your mouth in time. And what comes out of your mouth on a regular basis determines what type of life you will live!

Matthew 12:34, ... *for out of the abundance of the heart the mouth speaketh.*

Before you ever activate a principle into your life, make sure it lines up with the Word of God.

Acts 17:10-11 (Amplified) *Now the brethren at once sent Paul and Silas away by night to Beroea; and when they arrived, they entered the synagogue of the Jews. (11) Now these* [**Jews**] *were better disposed and more noble than those in Thessalonica, for they were entirely ready and accepted and welcomed the message* [**concerning the attainment through Christ of eternal salvation in the kingdom of God**] *with inclination of mind and eagerness, searching and examining the Scriptures daily to see if these things were so.*

What were these noble believers searching and examining daily? *The Scriptures!* Why? *They wanted to determine if Paul and Silas were telling the Truth.* You should always do the same, whenever you hear the Word of God proclaimed.

2) Note taking will help you gain a better understanding of what is being taught.

Understanding is a very important principle and topic in the Word of God. It will do you no good to hear the Word and then not understand how to apply that Word into your life. You will only be able to keep that portion of the Word that you understand.

> **Matthew 13:18-19,** *Hear ye therefore the parable of the sower. (19) When any one heareth the word of the kingdom, and understandeth it not, then cometh the wicked one, and catcheth away that which was sown in his heart. This is he which received seed by the way side.*

> *The devil does not want you to know the Word of God or how to use it because he knows the Word of God is the key to his defeat and your victory over him in every area of your life.*

> **Luke 24:45,** *Then opened he their understanding, that they might understand the scriptures.*

It is God's will that you understand His purpose and plan for your life. Note taking will assist you in this area. Schoolteachers today still use this system of teaching. When a teacher has a rule that they want a student to understand or remember, they often make that student write that particular rule a number of times. Unfortunately this system of teaching was often implemented when a violation of a rule occurred. The teacher felt that the violation occurred either because the

10

student did not understand the rule fully, or did not remember the rule. The solution to this dilemma was to have the student write the rule 100 to 500 times on a piece of paper. Have you ever had to do that? You cannot follow an instruction correctly that you do not fully understand. David gained understanding of the Will of God by writing things down.

I Chronicles 28:19, *All this, said David, the Lord made me understand in writing by his hand upon me, even all the works of this pattern.*

Proverbs 24:3 also declares that a house is built by wisdom, and by understanding it is established (paraphrased). You are the house of God, so begin taking notes at church. This type of dedication will increase your potential to fully understand what is being taught. *Understanding the Word of God is a step toward being established in the Word of God.*

3) Notes are written in the present for use in the future.

Isaiah 30:8 *Now go, write it before them in a table, and note it in a book, that it may be for the time to come for ever and ever:*

At the moment you become a citizen in the Kingdom of God by receiving Jesus Christ as your personal Lord and Savior, you become an enemy of Satan and subject to immediate attack. Every believer is involved in spiritual warfare of some sort. Our only offensive weapon in this spiritual war is the Word of God. Although there are many principles in the Word of God, your success will be determined by your ability to use the correct principle,

11

directed toward the situation or circumstance you want to change in your life.

The five-fold ministry (Apostles, Prophets, Evangelists, Pastors, and Teachers) (**Ephesians 4:11**), was given to equip you for this war and bring you to a state of spiritual maturity (**Ephesians 4:12-13**).

Are you a person who goes to Church at least two times a week? If you are, there are many different subjects pertaining to the Kingdom of God that you will encounter. Due to this fact, it would be to your advantage to take notes during every training session, not only to protect yourself against future attacks, but also to familiarize yourself with the benefits you are entitled to as a Christian. *No man on earth right now is the sum total of all knowledge, but a smart man will store knowledge to be activated when needed.*

What Is a Note?

I believe that before you will ever be successful in taking notes effectively, your understanding of what a note is must be secure. When I was receiving thoughts for this book, the main definition that stuck with me was this: Notes are stored information. Notes are information you desire to store or keep for whatever reason. Because our focus is related to that of a church service and the things you should do when you attend, it is important that you view these definitions in the light of that thought.

What is a note?

1. *Notes are stored information*
2. *Notes are brief records written down to aid the memory*
3. *Notes are informal or short messages written to trigger or influence your thought process*
4. *Notes are written explanations*

To add to these four definitions, I want to give you the Hebrew definition of this word, taken from the New Strong's Exhaustive Concordance of the Bible, authored by James Strong:

Note (H2710) A primitive root; properly to hack, that is engrave (Judges 5:14, to be a scribe simply); by implication to enact (laws being cut in *stone or metal tablets in primitive times) or (generally) <u>prescribe</u>*

The very last word that defines the word "note" is "prescribe." When I think of the word "prescribe" I think of a physician giving his patient a prescription. And a prescription is nothing more than a note given to you from your doctor to give to a pharmacist. This intensifies my desire to take notes even more. Why? Because it is recorded in the Bible three times that Jesus indirectly refers to Himself as a physician (**Matthew 9:12, Mark 2:17, Luke 5:31**).

A prescription, which is a note from your doctor, is normally given to you because you need some type of medicine or medical treatment for a fleshly (physical) problem. This is interesting as well in helping us to understand what a note is, because the Word of God is also called the Holy SCRIPTures. Let's look at **Proverbs 4:20-22**,

> *My son, attend to my words (preSCRIPTions); incline thine ear unto my sayings. Let them (preSCRIPTions) not depart from thine eyes; keep them in the midst of thine heart. For they (preSCRIPTions) are life unto those that find them, and <u>health (literally medicine) to all their flesh</u>.*

Nine Things You Should Always Write When Taking Notes At Church

One of the biggest things that motivated me in wanting to get the Body of Christ some information concerning "what" they should write when taking notes was watching my wife take notes. It was kind of funny because her passion and desire to get the things of God inside her was and still is remarkable. You could say she has a zeal for learning about God. When taking notes, my wife Chandra would attempt to write down everything that was said. As this action progressed, I would begin telling her to simply write portions of the message and I would buy the tape from the bookstore after the service. I did this in an attempt not to discourage her nor to belittle her effort, but to get her to recognize all the information she was missing while trying to write everything down. Let me say this to everyone: "**Romans 10:17** reveals how faith comes, BY HEARING," and it did not say by writing things down. _Hearing the Word of God proclaimed is the only way faith comes_.

When you are taking notes at church, if you are not selective on what you should write, then chances are you will miss something you should have heard that could have changed or impacted your life in a supernatural way. As time went on, my wife began to write selective portions of the message, with the understanding that I would purchase the tape.

My wife and I like to listen to tapes on a daily basis. This is an activity that we not only do together, but alone as well. One year, while serving in the tape ministry at my church, I was asked to go over some tapes. They simply wanted me to write the name of the person speaking, date of the tape, time of the tape, all the scriptures given on the tape, and a few things the minister talked about during the service. My wife wanted to help me because I had hundreds of tapes to go over, so I gave her a few tapes and told her about the assigned format.

I began to notice that it would take weeks for her to finish a few tapes, when I was finishing five to seven tapes a day. We both were in the habit of taking notes for ourselves along with filling out the already formatted paperwork given to us. Then one day while I was looking at her notebook I noticed the amount of information she was writing and it was a lot. I recognized that she went back to her old practice, where she felt it necessary to write almost the entire tape. This was to me a very admirable thing to do, but it does not mean it is the correct or most effective thing to do. I knew that whenever you attempt to give people new information that could come in the form of a correction, you needed to be very careful. So I was.

Sometimes when taking notes you can focus on a good thing, and it still is the wrong thing. My objective was to encourage my wife to continue what she was doing, while at the same time modify it in such a way that the knowledge God wanted her to hear at church would be heard. What I mean by that is, there is specific information that God desires for you to have whenever you attend church, or listen to the Word of God. Our misunderstanding of this sometimes leads us to believe that the extra information given to explain a biblical principle is the information God wanted us to have. It is good to remember, and sometimes even write down, the testimonies and examples given by the minister during the service, but we must always remember *that the testimonies and examples are normally given to bring clarity and understanding to the principle that is being discussed. We should never ever focus so much on getting the testimony and example in our notes that we forget or do not get the principle.* This is why I have provided nine things that I believe every uncommon Christian should write when taking notes, but remember always to let the Holy Spirit be your guide!

Always write:

1. The person's name who is teaching:

This will simply give you a point of reference and it may also trigger your memory or give assistance to your thought process when you are trying to recall something.

Always write:

2. The date of the lesson:

The same explanations for point number one can be used for point number two.

Always write:

3. The title or subject:

I believe this is very important. Every conversation that you will ever have will always involve a specific topic. In most cases the title or subject given will always reveal the topic of conversation. Of course, knowing the topic or subject will not only add to your potential in understanding the information given, but will also increase your opportunity in being a participant in the conversation.

Always write:

4. The purpose, objective, and goal for the particular teaching being taught:

I have been fortunate to be around a Pastor who always gives the purpose, objective, and goal for a particular teaching. The title or subject tells you "what" is going to be discussed. The purpose, objective, and goal reveal the "why" it is discussed. This should help you follow along, because the knowledge of this will ensure that everyone is going in the same direction.

Always write:

5. Every Scripture given to you:

In any service, the Word of God should be the most important information given. Every teaching you receive should always be based on the Scriptures. Jesus said that the sower sows the Word (**Mark 4:14**) and the place where the seed is sown is in your heart (**Mark 4:15**). So for me the most important part of the lesson is the Scriptures/Word of God that is being used, how it is being used, and how to apply it appropriately to my life and situations. **Mark 16:20** says God confirms His Word with signs following (paraphrased), not a man or a woman, but His Word. If this is true, and it is, then there is a connection between His Word and the signs that follow. Most of these signs are revealed in **Mark 16:17-18**:

And <u>these signs</u> shall follow them that believe; (sign) In my name shall they cast out devils; (sign) they shall speak with new tongues; (sign) They shall take up serpents; and if they drink any deadly thing, (sign) it shall not hurt them; (sign) they shall lay hands on the sick, and (sign) they shall recover.

That is enough to prove to me that the Word of God is very important. He only confirms His Word with signs following.

Another reason why you should write every scripture down is because you want to check to make sure that what you are being taught is correct, given in the proper context, and is taught line upon line, precept upon precept, here a little, there a little (**Isaiah 28:10**). If you can read, have a Bible, have the Holy Spirit living on the inside of you, and are willing to study, then the chances of someone deceiving you are slim to none.

The next three things that you should always write down when taking notes are what I call the body of your notes. These three things make up the majority of everything that you will ever note during the service.

Always write:

6. *That which "defines":*

> *Key Thought-* The ability to define increases the potential to fulfill.

That which *"defines"* means you are to write in your notebook when the minister:
- States the precise meaning of a word or phrase
- Describes the nature or basic qualities of something
- Explains the character of something

Always write:

7. *That which "informs":*

> *Key Thought-* Ignorance is dangerous because it permits the possibility that we will live all our lives and never know why we lived (*Myles Munroe*).

That which *"informs"* means you are to write in your notebook when the minister:
- Imparts information about a principle in the Word of God that you were not previously aware of
- Discloses incriminating information about you or a particular lifestyle you have chosen to participate in, not knowing God was against it

Incriminating information is information given to you by the minister/teacher that:

1. Agrees with the Word of God
2. Reveals violations you have made or are thinking about making
3. Reveals wrongful actions that exist in your life
4. Reveals to you knowledge that is pertinent to a successful Christian life

Always write:

8. That which "instructs"

Key Thought- Instruction involves wisdom, because it is the teaching of the application of knowledge. **Faith comes by hearing, but wisdom comes by asking!**

That which *"instructs"* means you are to write in your notebook when the minister:

- Provides you with knowledge in a methodical way
- Gives orders to you in the form of instructions
- Gives direction to you

Always write:

9. Any Word, command, or assignment the Lord speaks to your heart through the teacher, a yielded vessel, or a still small voice within you:

Exodus 20:1-3, *And God spake all these words, saying, (2) I am the Lord thy God, which have brought thee out of the land of Egypt, out of the*

house of bondage. (3) Thou shalt have no other gods before Me.

There are many different reasons why people attend church. Some attend because they want to show off their clothes, while others attend because they are looking for a mate. As strange as it may seem, some people attend church because someone made them go, and to keep the peace they went. I really can write a chapter on the wrong reasons why people go to church, but that is not the focus of this book. In **Exodus 20:2**, the Word of God declares that God is the Deliverer (and He is), then in **verse 3** He begins to give you the reasons why He made that statement: (**verse 3**) *Thou shalt have no other gods before me*. <u>God and your relationship with Him should be the number one reason why anyone attends church</u>. Church is a training ground and it is the place where the Will, Knowledge, Desire, and the Operation of God and the Kingdom of God are given.

Ironically, it was at church where God first spoke to me (a still small voice within) about the information contained in this book. The thoughts behind this book came to me first, while I was voluntarily serving in a helps ministry. If I had ignored the Word of God given to me at that time, my assignment for this book would have been transferred to another. I look forward to God the Father using me, and you should as well. But if you want God to use you, you must come to church prepared and EXPECTING GOD to give you a word, command, or assignment through whatever channel He uses. Once this is given to you, write it down immediately, because *one word from God can change your life forever!*

MARKING IN YOUR BIBLE

*Marking in your Bible is not an act of mutilation,
but an act of love.*

(Author Unknown)

The focus of this book is notetaking and constructive marking in your Bible is a form of notetaking. The purpose behind this form of notetaking is to help you become more familiar with your Bible, which would ultimately lead to a greater understanding of the Scriptures. God is not against you marking in your Bible. What God is against is you rejecting Him and His Words (**Hosea 4:6**). The Word of God is that which sustains life and the Word of God is the weapon you must use to bring victory into your own life (**Matthew 4:4, Ephesians 6:17**).

The Bible contains 3,566,489 letters, 810,697 words, 31,175 verses, 1,189 chapters, and 66 books. Your level of peace in life will be measured by your knowledge of the Word of God along with your ability to apply that knowledge to the different situations of your life. Some people are truly afraid to write anything in their Bible. For some reason, people believe that writing in their Bible is destructive, abusive, and disrespectful to God. If this thinking is correct, then let me ask you a question: How is it O.K. for a man or woman of God to reprint a Bible and have the publisher or editor include their comments, (called commentaries), on pages of the Bible? Did they get a permission slip from God? No, they did not, but if they can comment or mark in the Bible, whether formally or informally, so can you! If you feel that the Bible you have is too expensive to mark in, then go out and buy yourself a less expensive Bible, where your notes will not be a problem.

You should design the system that you use to mark in your Bible. This section of the book is simply to give you an example to follow or a blueprint to developing your own system. There are some tools you will need for marking in your Bible. I have listed them below:

- A Bible: everyone should own a Bible (never come to church without it)
- Pens
- Highlighters
- Hard square card or short ruler

The reason why I use these particular tools is because I believe you should be as neat as possible when marking in your Bible. Remember, God does all things *"decent"* and *"in order"* (**I Corinthians 14:40**, paraphrased). In the front of your Bible or the back of your Bible, wherever you can find an empty page, you will need to develop a highlighter color chart and a pen-marking chart.

For example:
- A yellow highlighter could be used to represent that which informs
- A blue highlighter could be used to represent that which instructs or commands you to do something
- A red pen could be used for underlining or arrows,

which would represent something very important you would want to remember

- A black pen could be used the same way as the red pen, but would represent the revealing of the kingdom of darkness and its devices
- And so on

As I said earlier, the colors or system you use is entirely up to you. You can also write definitions of words next to the word, and develop your own cross-references to Scriptures by writing the Scriptures next to it. There are many things you can do that would be very productive to you becoming more familiar with the Word of God.

WHAT DO I DO AFTER
I TAKE MY NOTES?

Hopefully, the information in this book has been a blessing to you up to this point. My intent has been to give you insight on "what" you should write when taking notes at church or wherever you have chosen to listen to the Word of God proclaimed. I am glad to say that many people take notes whether they know what to write or not. Therefore, the next piece of information that I am led to share with you is, *What you should do with your notes after you take them.* This information is given to you because I believe you desire to use the notes you take.

1. Take notes at church in a notebook.
2. Go back over your notes at home to make sure the information you received was correct.
3. Separate your notes by re-writing them in other notebooks you have personalized according to a particular subject (*Ex. Faith, Grace, Prayer, etc.*).
4. Systematically type your rewritten notes out and place them in subject binders.
5. Run copies to store in a file cabinet.
6. Input into your computer if you have one. (*this step can be done when you type them out*).
7. Place information into your daily meditation rotation.
8. Become the thought behind the note that you wrote (**BE A DOER OF THE WORD**).

9. Pass on the information to someone else.

Some people might be wondering, "Why should I go through all this work?" Let me make it very simple, the devil did not come to bother you, he did not come to make you unhappy, sick, poor, or frustrated. The devil is coming after you for one reason and one reason only: to KILL YOU!

John 10:10 *The thief cometh not, but for to steal, and to kill, and to destroy...*

As citizens of the Kingdom of God, we need to stop playing church and become the Church. To do this we must replace the majority of our learned behavior with Kingdom behavior. Please don't be lazy; make the extra effort to get what you need to get, so that you can be a blessing to someone else. If you did not know it, *"ministry"* is spelled "WORK." If this book has truly been a blessing to you, then use it as a manual or a guidebook to help you become a better student of the Word of God.

2 Timothy 2:15, *Study to shew thyself approved unto God, a workman that needeth not to be ashamed, rightly dividing the word of truth.*

Always remember that Jesus truly loves you, the knowledge that He shares with you at church is not for Him but for you. May God the Father forever bless you with the wisdom to know what to do with it, in Jesus' name.

Thank you for reading,

Ralph Smith

ABOUT THE AUTHOR

Ralph Smith is a man of God who is dedicated to the call of God on his life. He has been recognized in many circles as an anointed man of God who teaches the Word of God with simplicity and power. Simply put, "his focus is His Focus." His true desire is to do the will of God, nothing more and nothing less. Ralph Smith is married with three children and currently resides in St. Louis, Missouri.

Ralph Smith
1124 New Florissant
St. Louis, MO 63135-1148

NOTES

NOTES

NOTES

_____

_____

_____

_____

_____

_____

_____

_____

_____

_____

_____

_____

_____

_____

_____

_____

_____

_____

_____

_____

NOTes

NOTES

NOTES

NOTES

_____

_____

_____

_____

_____

_____

_____

_____

_____

_____

_____

_____

_____

_____

_____

_____

_____

_____

_____

_____

_____

NOTES

NOTES

NOTES

NOTES

NOTES

NOTES

_____

_____

_____

_____

_____

_____

_____

_____

_____

_____

_____

_____

_____

_____

_____

_____

_____

_____

_____

_____

_____

_____

_____